TEMPLE

The British Haiku Society Members' Anthology
2021

**The British Haiku
Society**

Founded 1990

Previous BHS Members' Anthologies:

1992	Sea		2007	Storm
1993	Fire		2008	Building
1994	Hill		2009	Earth
1995	Sky		2010	Celebration
1996	Home		2011	Gift
1997	Away		2012	Air
1998	Island		2013	Time
1999	Forest		2014	Sound
2000	Space		2015	Edge
2001	Flat		2016	Beginning
2002	Hidden		2017	Ekphrasis
2003	Path		2018	Wild
2004	Other		2019	Root
2005	River		2020	City
2006	Light			

Introduction

This year's anthology truly reflects the international character of our society – a record-breaking 196 BHS members from Australia, Brazil, Bulgaria, Canada, Denmark, France, Germany, India, Ireland, Israel, Italy, Japan, Luxembourg, Malta, The Netherlands, New Zealand, Portugal, Romania, Russia, Sweden, Switzerland, UK, and USA submitted their haiku and tanka. Over 40 poets have kindly added translations in their mother tongue or in the language spoken in their adopted country.

I would like to thank those who contributed with their poems and all BHS members for their continued support over the years. Your enthusiastic response, kind messages and good wishes are much appreciated. My special thanks to Caroline Skanne for selecting my haiku and for proofreading the anthology!

Haikai poetry is our temple!

Iliyana Stoyanova
October 2021

Sheila Windsor, UK

abbey gardens the cabbage-white closes her wings

Jo Balistreri, USA

a chair, a smoke
my fishing hole on North Cedar
in the deep peace of ice

Michael Dylan Welch, USA

a deer in the mist . . .
the forest light
at Seabeck

* *Seabeck* is a small scenic town on the Kitsap peninsula between Seattle, Washington and the snow-capped Olympic mountains. The conference centre there is home to the annual Seabeck Haiku Getaway. (*author's note*)

Radhamani Sarma, India

after all misdeeds
introspect by atonement
heart full of idols
this warring soul worships
after year-long pricks and pains

Pearl Elizabeth Dell May, UK

A golden beauty
dedicated to worshipping
how could you not pray

Alison Williams, UK

a high arch
where the tree tops meet
each time a sense
of passage
to the other side

Anna Eklund-Cheong, France

all the world's problems
solved before dessert…
kitchen table

Alexandar Dabnishki, Bulgaria

A man
leaned against a column.
Who does keep the dome up?

Човек
облегнат на колона.
Кой купола горе държи?

(Bulgarian trans. by Alexandar Dabnishki)

Madhuri Pillai, Australia

ancestral home
in the jasmine-scented twilight
old caretaker's chant

Pat Geyer, USA

an old shanty church
leans into the setting sun…
no one says a prayer

Marie Therese Truong-von Rohr, Luxembourg

an old wooden bench
and bubbling river
a prayer to the clouds

un vieux banc en bois
et le clapotis de la rivière
une prière aux nuages

(French trans. by Marie Therese Truong)

Keith J. Coleman, UK

an umbrella
half closed around her   through the blizzard
a muffled bell

Caroline Skanne, UK

a path into another path gatekeeper

en väg till en annan väg buskgräsfjäril

(Swedish trans. by Caroline Skanne)

Bill Shannon, UK

a Sabbath afternoon
in the sycamores
a parliament of rooks

Iliyana Stoyanova, UK

as if
drawn by a child
Mt Fuji

сякаш
нарисувана от дете
Фуджи-сан

(Bulgarian trans. by Iliyana Stoyanova)

Malcolm Williams, UK

a single dried daisy
bisects
The Book of Psalms

Graham High, UK

awaiting blossom
the cherry tree gnarled with age;
the place of worship

Basem Farid, UK

baptizing the infant
in the font
a rubber duck

Nancy Shires, USA

bar mitzvah
after the rabbi's monotone
dancing the horah

* *Horah* (Hebrew והרה) — a type of circle dance widespread in the Jewish diaspora; at b'nai mitzvah it is customary to raise the honouree, and sometimes his or her family members, on a chair during the horah.

Neil Somerville, UK

Before
Behind
Beyond
OM

Michael Flanagan, USA

beside our candle
as it flickers orange and blue
your breath on my face

Diarmuid Fitzgerald, Ireland

beside the busy road
raked pebbles
in deep silence

in aice an bothar gnóthach
púróga scuaibe
í tost domhain

(Irish trans. by Diarmuid Fitzgerald)

Jon Iddon, UK

between blooms
morning cobwebs cradle
the mist

Corine Timmer, Portugal

between the beats of the drums everything and nothing

tussen de slagen van de trommen alles en niks

(Dutch trans. by Corine Timmer)

Tony Williams, UK

beyond my bed
the soft chatter
of autumn rain

M. Shayne Bell, USA

blue herons
wading in watered fields…
dusk

Beverly Acuff Momoi, USA

bowing
to the muse
wisteria

Mary Burgess, UK

bread held aloft
as tinkling bells signify change
salvation

Wyntirson, UK

breathing in the chime my heart

Derek Sprecksel, USA

Bruckner's Ninth
news of a close friend's
untimely passing

Rick Wilson, USA

buried by a landslide
partly reconstructed
still inspiring

Sue Richards, UK

bust of Mithras…
a Roman snail holds tight
between cracked stones

* *Mithraism* (also known as the Mithraic mysteries) – the cult of god
Mithras, carried and supported by the Imperial Roman army (1st-4th
century AD).

Lorraine Haig, Australia

butcherbird
its song trickles
into the pond

Kath Abela Wilson, USA

call to prayer
our international collab
at Hotel Poem

* *Hotel Poem* in Istanbul, Turkey, where my husband Rick and I stayed
on our visit in 2010, is situated just a short walk from Hagia Sophia
and Blue Mosque, overlooking the Bosphorus. (*author's note*)

Diana Webb, UK

Candlemas
a sprinkling of snowdrops
around the dovecote

Felicity Denby, UK

Cathedral candles
still light, still life, still our lives:
prayers ascending

Susan Lee Kerr, UK

centred
Jacob wrestles the angel
in pink polished stone

Robert Kingston, UK

chantry chapel
the long hmmm
at the closed sign

Zornitza Harizanova, Bulgaria

Christmas Eve
making a wish upon
the brightest star…

Бъдни вечер
отправям желание
към най-ярката звезда…

(Bulgarian trans. by Zornitza Harizanova)

Christopher Peys, USA

church cry-room
an infant speaks
in tongues

Bryan Rickert, USA

churchyard squirrel
its praying hands
around a nut

Tito, Japan

Clinking wooden plaques
now on its way
over diamond stepping stones…
the spring breeze

(Manpukuji, Uji, 19.4.21)

Ron C. Moss, Australia

cloudy summit
sitting in the silence
of becoming

Alan Maley, UK

commemoration:
hot air fills the cathedral –
was this really him?

Keith Sherman, UK

cool autumn sunlight
filtering through the trees
an ethereal haze
softens the ragged remains
of plundered priory walls

Susanna Rivière, UK

cushion
and candle flame –
my breathing settles

Ruth Parker, UK

dawn in the forest
all around
choir practice

Marilyn Ashbaugh, USA

dawn zikr
the robin bows
to the worm

* *Zikr* (Arabic: ذِكْر – 'reminding oneself' or 'mention') is a ritual prayer or litany practised by Sufis (Muslim mystics) for the purpose of glorifying God and achieving spiritual perfection.

Debbi Antebi, UK

deep forest
the words of a prayer
I once knew

Mary Kendall, USA

deep in meditation
I am no bigger than
a single grain of sand
so easily forgotten,
so easily overlooked

Nancy Richards, Canada

deep in the woods
a log, an owl
and my thoughts

Julie Thorndyke, Australia

dense shade
fills this cathedral of ferns
an ancient light
beams through green silences
and the tracery of primeval life

Leo Lavery, UK

deserted farmhouse
ferns
in the fireplace

Erica Ison, UK

deserted shrine
a bell rings
to summon the spirits

Nola Turner, UK

dogs howl at noon
among ancient stones
Baal in smithereens

* The *Temple of Baal* (Arabic: بل مع بد) – located in Palmyra, Syria, founded in AD 32, destroyed by the ISIS in August 2015; reconstruction began in 2021.

William Scott Galasso, USA

Dome of the Rock
a twinkling brightness
drawn by stars

Mattias Granfrid, Sweden

during meditation
I suddenly remember
why

under meditationen
minns jag plötsligt
varför

(Swedish trans. by Mattias Granfrid)

Amanda Bell, Ireland

dusk falls early –
silhouettes of apples
through stained glass

titeann an oíche go luath –
scáthchruthanna na n-úll
trí ghloine dhaite

(Irish trans. by Gabriel Rosenstock)

Gary Hittmeyer, USA

dusty hymnals
the congregation scattered
like leaves

Claire Vogel Camargo, USA

each stone
placed with a murmur
prayer cairn

Graham Duff, UK

early mist and drizzle
inside the long barrow
incense and dolls

Carol Quentin-Hicks, UK

early morning
a peregrine swoops
from the amber spire

Bill Cooper, USA

Easter cantata
the choirmaster begs me
to lip sync

Charles Christian, UK

East Somerton Church…
tumbled walls, roofless
…the witch leg touches the sky

* The legend on the church of St Mary's East Somerton (on the Norfolk Broads near Great Yarmouth) is many centuries ago a witch with a wooden leg was buried alive in the church foundations; with her dying breath she cursed the church and her wooden leg subsequently grew into the oak tree that now grows up through the roofless ruins of the church. (*author's note*)

Humberto Gatica, UK

empty church
the pain on a whispering
from a confession chamber

en la Iglesia vacía
un doloroso susurro
desde el confesionario

(Spanish trans. by Humberto Gatica)

David Bingham, UK

end of mass…
snuffing out
the altar candles

Michele Root-Bernstein, USA

evening chores
crickets sing the darkness
out of the long grass

Linda Sadler, UK

eyes closed
sinking further and further
all that is

Colin Oliver, UK

fading to dusk
in the mirror font
the roof angels

Klaus-Dieter Wirth, Germany

feeling lonely
so thin the sound
of the chapel's bell

sich einsam fühlen
so dünn der Klang des Glöckchens
von der Kapelle

(German trans. by Klaus-Dieter Wirth)

Caroline Robson, UK

first date
a carol concert
holding hands

Auricéia Dumke, Brazil

following the light
the moon's been showing the way
finally... in paradise

em direção da luz
o luar mostra o caminho
finalmente... no paraíso

(Brazilian Portuguese trans. by Auricéia Dumke)

Katherine Gallagher, UK

following the river
wondering
where it will end

David J Kelly, Ireland

forest glade
a fox scat on the altar
of a tree trunk

Jill Lange, USA

from the hands
that carved St.Francis
this ginkgo seedling

Maureen Edden, UK

frost on the dome
my hands frozen
in prayer

Dennis Tomlinson, UK

golden deer
on the wall of the wat
    the gates still locked

Sue Lewis, UK

gold statues
rich smoke of yak butter

Addison Redley, UK

grave stones
linear order
unlike life

Derek Hughes, UK

grey sky
grey sea
distant lights

Roger Noons, UK

habit forming…
visiting the monk's
cemetery

Diane Davy, UK

harbouring longings
to see his lovely face beaming
fresh flowers by his photo

Jim Curry, UK

harvesting
the allotment
time to share

Charlotte Bigg, UK

head in hands
musing on the world at large
where did prayers go wrong?

Marion New, UK

her body sways
notes fly from the violin
around Doric pillars

Pete Dunstone, UK

Holy Island
seals surface and submerge
in the seaweed

* *Holy Island* or the *Holy Island of Iona* lies off the west coast of Mull in the Inner Hebrides. St Columba landed here from Ireland founding an Abbey and bringing Christianity to Scotland in the 6th century. (*author's note*)

Paul Bregazzi, Ireland

hurrying monk —
below his habit
the Nike swoosh

fuadar mhanaigh —
faoin a aibíd
siosarnach Nike

(Irish trans. by Ailín Bregazzi)

Carita Forslund, Sweden

hymn of the day
I raise my hands
to pick a cherry

dagens lovsång
jag sträcker upp händerna
och plockar ett körsbär

(Swedish trans. by Carita Forslund)

Carole MacRury, USA

if there is a god
she's here in the forest
teaching me
to embrace my shadow
along with the light

Geoffrey Winch, UK

incense
at the edge of the woods
the spirit moves

Damian Stanford-Harris, UK

Incense softness
Cedarwood smoothness –
In the sighing spaces of the dark
The Buddha

Paul Hickey, UK

in silence
walking meditation
a sanctuary

Maya Daneva, The Netherlands

intercession
the spoken and
the unspoken

застъпническа молитва
казаното и
неизказаното

(Bulgarian trans. by Maya Daneva and Iliyana Stoyanova)

Patricia Prime, New Zealand

in the cathedral
the violinist's fingertips
caress his instrument

Marilyn Humbert, Australia

in the park
beneath my bodhi tree
I find peace
in chittering birds
and the rustling leaves

Dick Pettit, Denmark

In the pub
after closing time
confidences
contemplation, perhaps:
you'd hardly call it prayer.

i værtshuset
efterfarvellerne
fortrolighed;
beskuelser, måske;
ærlig talt, det er ikke bøn

(Danish trans. by Dick Pettit)

frances angela, UK

in the shade of trees by the river waking as the geese leave

Roger Watson, UK

lakeside chapel
a swallow's nest
in the porch

Radostina Dragostinova, Bulgaria

learning self-hugging
dandelion in the storm

да се научиш сам да се прегръщаш
глухарче в бурята

(Bulgarian trans. by Radostina Dragostinova)

Mona Iordan, Romania

library room
the city bustle
miles away

sala de lectură
zarva oraşului
la leghe depărtare

(Romanian trans. by Mona Iordan)

Veronica A. Shimanovskaya, USA

light is falling askance
dancing in all the corners
my rainbow room

света косые лучи
танцуют повсюду
моя комната радуг

(Russian trans. by Veronica A. Shimanovskaya)

Sarah Lawson, UK

Light slanting through leaves
dappled on the forest floor—
The crunch of footsteps

Radu Şerban, Romania

liturgical songs –
under the cathedral porch
swallow chicks chirping

liturgic melos –
sub scocul catedralei
puii de lăstun

(*Romanian trans. by Radu Şerban*)

Katja Fox, UK

lonely alpine walks
tinkling cow bells send prayers
I give the dog a home

Chris Luck, UK

lover of dark places
the wren's whole body trembles
when it sings

Helen May Williams, UK

Lundy & Caldey
float on marine light
upturned coracle halos

Ynys Wair ac Ynys Bŷr
golau mar arnofiol
cwryglau corongylch

(*Welsh trans. by Helen May Williams*)

* *Lundy* is an island in the Bristol Channel; it forms part of the district of Torridge in the county of Devon. Its Welsh name refers to the wizard Gwydion, whose name means 'born of trees'. *Caldey* (Welsh: Ynys Bŷr) is a small island off Tenby, Pembrokeshire, Wales. Inhabited since the Neolithic era, a Celtic Monastery was established there in the 6th century. To this day, a community of Cistercian monks lives in the Abbey on what is considered one of Britain's holy isles. (*author's note*)

Lee Gurga, USA

materializing
matins

vespers
whispers

Roberta Beary, Ireland

memorial mass
the part my brother
always sang

Barbara Tate, USA

midnight fog
the lighthouse beacon
a wide arc of warning

Carol Mayer, UK

miniature Stonehenge
long view over the dale
bilberry bushes

Debbie Strange, Canada

moon bridge
the arch of a dragonfly
laying eggs

Carol Raisfeld, USA

morning meditation
on warm sand
waves of silence

Liam Maguire, UK

morning prayers… the birds begin their daily devotions

Deborah Karl-Brandt, Germany

mountain hike
in the limestone rubble
the ancient sea

Bergwanderung
im Kalksteinschutt
das Urmeer

(German trans. by Deborah Karl-Brandt)

Karen Hoy, UK

my health and safety the gatekeeper butterfly

Nikolay Grankin, Russia

nightingale trill
i move my late father's chair
to the window

соловьиная трель
подвигаю к окну кресло
покойного отца

(*Russian trans. by Nikolay Grankin*)

Sean O'Connor, Ireland

night meditation…
the kane resounding
beyond the stars

* *kane* (鉦) is a Japanese meditation bell. (*author's note*)

Vanessa Proctor, Australia

ocean at sunrise
diving beneath
wave after wave

Blaine Ward, UK

on a certain flagstone
Eight Strands of the Brocade
rain, hail or shine

* *Eight Strands of the Brocade* or The Baduanjin qigong (八段錦) is one of the most common forms of Chinese qigong used as exercise. The name of the form generally refers to how the eight individual movements of the form characterize and bestow a silken quality to the body and its energy.

Marc Evans, UK

Only the wind
attempts the ritual chant –
vacant stadium

Dim ond y gwynt
yn suo-ganu'r emyn-donau
mewn stadiwm gwag

(Welsh trans. by Marc Evans)

John Gonzalez, UK

opening doors –
suddenly
a carpet of light

Kate B Hall, UK

outside for the day
sunshine but no writing book
I write on an old pill packet

Andrew Shimield, UK

over the headstone
a magnolia bends
in a bower of blossom

Topher Dykes, UK

pad 39
experiencing satori
one small step

* *Pad 39* was the launch facility, at Kennedy Space Centre, where the Apollo lunar missions departed from. (*author's note*)

Bakhtiyar Amini, Germany

pagoda
Buddha listens to me
smiling

пагода
слушает меня Будда
с улыбкой

(Russian trans. by Bakhtiyar Amini)

Simon Williams, UK

pale dusty sunlight
tiptoes up the ancient steps
warms the crumbling stones
a million pilgrims passing
have all beheld this same dawn

Martin Caley, UK

parish church
under the Christmas tree
forgotten tombs

Janette Ostle, UK

petals open
anointing the morning
dewdrops

Ann Rawson, UK

piercing
the ancient cromlech
rays of sunshine

a' bioradh
na crom-lic' àrsaidh
gathan grèine

(Scottish Gaelic trans. by Marcas Mac an Tuairneir)

Deborah P Kolodji, USA

prayer hands
the forest canopy
bathed in light

Akito Mori, Japan

Praying…
with equinox flowers
for autumn tomb

秋分に　墓のお参り　彼岸花

(Japanese trans. by Akito Mori)

Kenneth Mullen, UK

rain dripping from hood
miniature eye-level land
soll moss seedling

rain draps frae bunnet
wee laund level wi' een
yird fogg plantie

(Scots trans. by Kenneth Mullen)

Rob Smallwood, UK

rain drips off the roof
and yet for the crowd inside
prayers as usual

Alan Peat, UK

raining ropes —
the moss garden softens
our edges

Jasmin Kirkbride, UK

raptor hangs on a lake breeze
diving for plastic scraps

John Hawkhead, UK

renewing vows
the sacred mystery
of why she chose me

Maeve O'Sullivan, Ireland

retreat centre the bee snuggles into a fuchsia

tearmann siortaíonn beach i ndeoir Dé

(*Irish trans. by Maeve O'Sullivan*)

Fred Schofield, UK

river running
    under a bridge   someone sings
        long and low

Roman Lyakhovetsky, Israel

roadside minyan
heavy bunches of dates
swaying in the wind

וינמ דצב דרדה
תולוכשא תודבכ לש םירמת
תודנדנתמ חורב

миньян у дороги —
тяжелые гроздья фиников
качаются на ветру

(Hebrew and Russian trans. by Roman Lyakhovetsky)

---

* *Minyan* (Hebrew: וינמ\נְמְיָן minyán [minˈjan], lit. count, number) in Judaism is the quorum of ten Jewish adults required for certain religious obligations, the most common activity being a public prayer.

Joy Heath, UK

rocky foreshore
our own
stone circle

John Rowlands, UK

Sacre Cœur
both unbelievers
we light candles

dau ddidduw
yn y Sacre Cœur
goleuwn ganhwyllau

(*Welsh trans. by John Rowlands*)

Rolf Baum, Sweden

safe among pine trees
their wide trunks embracing me
as light sifts through the crowns

skyddad av tallar
stammar som omsluter mig
kronorna silar ljuset

(Swedish trans. by Rolf Baum)

Victoria Gatehouse, UK

salvation yard –
an angel with chipped wings
to watch over us

Richard Thomas, UK

same rock
different river
silver carp wake

David Cobb, UK
(1926-2020)

scarecrow in church –
how wide the pleading arms,
how stiff the knees!

(first publ. in *Spring Journey to the Saxon Shore*, Equinox Press, 1997)

Erica Benson, UK

sheep safely shelter
behind the Stones of Stenness
curlews swerve storm clouds

Paul Beech, UK

shining deep
in cyber space
a haiku blog …
I listen for waves
between words

Brendon Kent, UK

shinrin yoku
everywhere
the sound of me

* *shinrin yoku* means 'forest bathing' or 'taking in the forest atmosphere' –
a mindfulness practice which emerged in Japan in the 1980s.

Ian Storr, UK

Shinto shrine
ah! the cream-filled pancakes
shaped like carp

Ian Hindmarch, UK

shrine of old sea gods
native girl brings fresh picked fruit
Xmas in Bali

Tim Gardiner, UK

sliding doors
who cares
who got away

Francis Attard, Malta

snake spirals in its coil of time
& its look of karma shapes
a crop circle
choral voices at daybreak
chanting matins

Tony Nasuta, USA

snow crunch
underfoot
prayer labyrinth

Hazel Hall, Australia

snow on snow
the toll of the bell
deeper now

Anna Maris, Sweden

sound of wind chimes
within lightness and darkness
lightness and darkness

ljudet av vindspel
i ljuset och mörkret
ljuset och mörkret

(*Swedish trans. by Anna Maris*)

Helen Buckingham, UK

sparrow
carolling
me home

Meg Arnot, UK

spring dawn
glints on the hilltop steeple
balm for troubled thoughts

Helen Buckingham, UK

sparrow
carolling
me home

Sue Beckwith, UK

stained glass rose windows
loud with sunset – crimson and gold
as Gaudi dreamt them

Daniela Misso, Italy

spring water –
weaving the silence
of a willow

acqua di sorgente –
tessendo il silenzio
di un salice

(*Italian trans. by Daniela Misso*)

Sheila K. Barksdale, UK

stained-glass window highlights all my pain

Nick T, UK

standing stones –
I breathe in
the silence

Bisshie, Switzerland

St Cecilia's day –
terracotta tiles
the rain beats on

* *Saint Cecilia* is a Roman martyr, celebrated by many Christian denominations on 22 November; she is the patron of music and musicians.

Clifford Rames, USA

still as a statue
a lizard fakes a mustache
across Buddha's lip

Teri White Carns, USA

stone Ganesh
in the reed-edged billabong
under snow gum trees
where your noon prayers and mine
whisper with north breezes

Marc May, The Netherlands

Stonehenge –
the weight of
a past belief

Stonehenge –
het gewicht van
een voorbij geloof

(*Dutch trans. by Marc May*)

Susan Beth Furst, USA

sukkah
through the palm branches
a starry night

* *sukkah* – a booth or hut in which the Jewish people eat and even sleep during the week-long celebration of Sukkot. The sukkah represents the huts in which the Jewish people dwelt in the desert when God brought them out of Egypt. It is decorated with seasonal fruits, and the roof is made of branches so the stars can be seen at night. (*author's note*)

karen robbie, UK

summer
in our small garden
dandelion wind

Richard L. Matta, USA

Sunday service
a cardinal chirps
between chants

Christine Eales, UK

Sunday worship
flooding out into the sunlight
after the storm

Gabriel Rosenstock, Ireland

sweltering heat . . .
shadows spend all afternoon
in the ruins

brothall . . .
an tráthnóna ar fad caite ag scáileanna
san fhothrach

(Irish trans. by Gabriel Rosenstock)

Freddy Ben-Arroyo, Israel

Tears and blood *sacred stones* in Jerusalem

בירושלים קדושות אבנים ודם דמעות

(*Hebrew trans. by Freddy Ben-Arroyo*)

A A Marcoff, UK

the blue shamanic
kingfisher
at the end of the river
where dreams
run wild

Hanne Hansen, Denmark

the bride from the city
married in the village church
does not change name

bruden fra byen
viet i landsbykirken
ændrer ikke navn

(*Danish trans. by Hanne Hansen*)

Peter Draper, UK

the holy table
bread and wine
and hand gel

Michael Fessler, Japan

the joinery
of the Mountain Gate
Soseki's koan

Wendy Toth Notarnicola, USA

the steady drone
of a bumblebee
morning mantra

Helen Gaen, UK

thoughts growing
and shrinking
garden cool

Alan Summers, UK

through the fields the dogs the humans the sky as birdsong

Tim Holland, UK

through the hole
in the sea wall –
slide show snaps

Peter Morriss, UK

to an open sky
high peaks
bare their fangs

Mark Gilfillan, UK

town square
the bell's first strike
a scatter of pigeons

Joanna Ashwell, UK

tree house
the forest becoming
a thatch of sunbeams

Olga Levitt, UK

tripping
between the buttercups
magpies

Frank Williams, UK

vespers
in the low-lit church
my candle flickers

Eufemia Griffo, Italy

vigil prayers
a hummingbird disappears
in the sunlight

veglia di preghiere
un colibrì scompare
nella luce del sole

(Italian trans. by Eufemia Griffo)

Julie Mellor, UK

votive candles
the warmth of your breath
haunting the dark

Sue Schraer, UK

walking backwards
the distance between
her and the Buddha

Robert Smith, UK

war memorial
the stone widow
eternally sorrowful

Alasdair Paterson, UK

wayfarers' church
the saint in pilgrim clothes
walking to his tomb

Mark Gilbert, UK

where the old pear tree stood collecting kindling

Marilyn Fleming, USA

white lotus
opening at dawn
OM mantra

Susan Spooner, Canada

woodland dusk
the birds sing
evensong

Susan King, UK

zazen —
an urge to scratch
where I shouldn't

Michael Smeer (Mikō), The Netherlands

zen garden
a shakuhachi fills
the midday heat

zen tuin
'n shakuhachi vult
de middaghitte

(Dutch trans. by Michael Smeer (Mikō)

* *shakuhachi* (Japanese: 尺八) – a traditional Japanese bamboo flute.
(*author's note*)

Index of Poets

A A Marcoff, UK – p.177
Addison Redley, UK – p.82
Akito Mori, Japan – p.136
Alan Maley, UK – p.47
Alan Peat, UK – p.139
Alan Summers, UK – p.183
Alasdair Paterson, UK – p.194
Alexandar Dabnishki, Bulgaria – p.11
Alison Williams, UK – p.9
Amanda Bell, Ireland – p.61
Andrew Shimield, UK – p.126
Ann Rawson, UK – p.132
Anna Eklund-Cheong, France – p.10
Anna Maris, Sweden – p.160
Auricéia Dumke, Brazil – p.75
Bakhtiyar Amini, Germany – p.128
Barbara Tate, USA – p.112
Basem Farid, UK – p.21
Beverly Acuff Momoi, USA – p.30
Bill Cooper, USA – p.66
Bill Shannon, UK – p.17
Bisshie, Switzerland – p.167
Blaine Ward, UK – p.122
Brendon Kent, UK – p.153

Bryan Rickert, USA – p.44
Carita Forslund, Sweden – p.91
Carol Mayer, UK – p.113
Carol Quentin-Hicks, UK – p.65
Carol Raisfeld, USA – p.115
Carole MacRury, USA – p.92
Caroline Robson, UK – p.74
Caroline Skanne, UK – p.16
Charles Christian, UK – p.67
Charlotte Bigg, UK – p.87
Chris Luck, UK – p.108
Christine Eales, UK – p.174
Christopher Peys, USA – p.43
Claire Vogel Camargo, USA – p.63
Clifford Rames, USA – p.168
Colin Oliver, UK – p.72
Corine Timmer, Portugal – p.27
Damian Stanford-Harris, UK – p.94
Daniela Misso, Italy – p.163
David Bingham, UK – p.69
David Cobb, UK – p.150
David J Kelly, Ireland – p.77
Debbi Antebi, UK – p.52
Debbie Strange, Canada – p.114

Deborah Karl-Brandt, Germany – p.117
Deborah P Kolodji, USA – p.135
Dennis Tomlinson, UK – p.80
Derek Hughes, UK – p.83
Derek Sprecksel, USA – p.33
Diana Webb, UK – p.38
Diane Davy, UK – p.85
Diarmuid Fitzgerald, Ireland – p.25
Dick Pettit, Denmark – p.99
Erica Benson, UK – p.151
Erica Ison, UK – p.57
Eufemia Griffo, Italy – p.190
Felicity Denby, UK – p.39
Frances Angela, UK – p.100
Francis Attard, Malta – p.157
Frank Williams, UK – p.189
Fred Schofield, UK – p.143
Freddy Ben-Arroyo, Israel – p.176
Gabriel Rosenstock, Ireland – p.175
Gary Hittmeyer, USA – p.62
Geoffrey Winch, UK – p.93
Graham Duff, UK – p.64
Graham High, UK – p.20
Hanne Hansen, Denmark – p.178
Hazel Hall, Australia – p.159
Helen Buckingham, UK – p.161
Helen Gaen, UK – p.182
Helen May Williams, UK – p.109
Humberto Gatica, UK – p.68

Ian Hindmarch, UK – p.155
Ian Storr, UK – p.154
Iliyana Stoyanova, UK – p.18
Janette Ostle, UK – p.131
Jasmin Kirkbride, UK – p.140
Jill Lange, USA – p.78
Jim Curry, UK – p.86
Jo Balistreri, USA – p.5
Joanna Ashwell, UK – p.187
John Gonzalez, UK – p.124
John Hawkhead, UK – p.141
John Rowlands, UK – p.146
Jon Iddon, UK – p.26
Joy Heath, UK – p.145
Julie Mellor, UK – p.191
Julie Thorndyke, Australia – p.55
Karen Hoy, UK – p.118
Karen Robbie, UK – p.172
Kate B Hall, UK – p.125
Kath Abela Wilson, USA – p.37
Katherine Gallagher, UK – p.76
Katja Fox, UK – p.107
Keith J. Coleman, UK – p.15
Keith Sherman, UK – p.48
Kenneth Mullen, UK – p.137
Klaus-Dieter Wirth, Germany – p.73
Lee Gurga, USA – p.110
Leo Lavery, UK – p.56
Liam Maguire, UK – p.116

Linda Sadler, UK – p.71

Lorraine Haig, Australia – p.36

M. Shayne Bell, USA – p.29

Madhuri Pillai, Australia – p.12

Maeve O'Sullivan, Ireland – p.142

Malcolm Williams, UK – p.19

Marc Evans, UK – p.123

Marc May, The Netherlands – p.170

Marie Therese Truong-von Rohr,
                    Luxembourg – p.14

Marietta McGregor, Australia – p.133

Marilyn Ashbaugh, USA – p.51

Marilyn Fleming, USA – p.196

Marilyn Humbert, Australia – p.98

Marion New, UK – p.88

Mark Gilbert, UK – p.195

Mark Gilfillan, UK – p.186

Martin Caley, UK – p.130

Mary Burgess, UK – p.31

Mary Kendall, USA – p.53

Mattias Granfrid, Sweden – p.60

Maureen Edden, UK – p.79

Maya Daneva, The Netherlands – p.96

Meg Arnot, UK – p.162

Michael Dylan Welch, USA – p.6

Michael Fessler, Japan – p.180

Michael Flanagan, USA – p.24

Michael Smeer (Mikō),
              The Netherlands – p.199

Michele Root-Bernstein, USA – p.70

Mona Iordan, Romania – p.103

Nancy Richards, Canada – p.54

Nancy Shires, USA – p.22

Neil Somerville, UK – p.23

Nick T, UK – p.166

Nikolay Grankin, Russia – p.119

Nola Turner, UK – p.58

Olga Levitt, UK – p.188

Padraig O'Morain, Ireland – p.134

Pat Geyer, USA – p.13

Patricia Prime, New Zealand – p.97

Paul Beech, UK – p.152

Paul Bregazzi, Ireland – p.90

Paul Hickey, UK – p.95

Pearl Elizabeth Dell May, UK – p.8

Pete Dunstone, UK – p.89

Peter Draper, UK – p.179

Peter Morriss, UK – p.185

Radhamani Sarma, India – p.7

Radostina Dragostinova,
                    Bulgaria – p.102

Radu Şerban, Romania – p.106

Richard L. Matta, USA – p.173

Richard Thomas, UK – p.149

Rick Wilson, USA – p.34

Rob Smallwood, UK – p.138

Robert Kingston, UK – p.41

Robert Smith, UK – p.193

Roberta Beary, Ireland – p.111
Roger Noons, UK – p.84
Roger Watson, UK – p.101
Rolf Baum, Sweden – p.147
Roman Lyakhovetsky, Israel – p.144
Ron C. Moss, Australia – p.46
Ruth Parker, UK – p.50
Sarah Lawson, UK – p.105
Sean O'Connor, Ireland – p.120
Sheila K. Barksdale, UK – p.165
Sheila Windsor, UK – p.4
Simon Williams, UK – p.129
Sue Beckwith, UK – p.164
Sue Lewis, UK – p.81
Sue Richards, UK – p.35
Sue Schraer, UK – p.192
Susan Beth Furst, USA – p.171
Susan King, UK – p.198

Susan Lee Kerr, UK – p.40
Susan Spooner, Canada – p.197
Susanna Riviere, UK – p.49
Teri White Carns, USA – p.169
Tim Gardiner, UK – p.156
Tim Holland, UK – p.184
Tito, Japan – p.45
Tony Nasuta, USA – p.158
Tony Williams, UK – p.28
Topher Dykes, UK – p.127
Vanessa Proctor, Australia – p.121
Veronica A. Shimanovskaya,
                                    USA – p.104
Victoria Gatehouse, UK – p.148
Wendy Toth Notarnicola, USA – p.181
William Scott Galasso, USA – p.59
Wyntirson, UK – p.32
Zornitza Harizanova, Bulgaria – p.42

Editor: Iliyana Stoyanova
Book layout: Iliyana Stoyanova
Cover: Photo by Iliyana Stoyanova; Graphic design by Sider Evtimov (SeeDesign Ltd)

ISBN: 978-1-906333-16-4

Published by:
The British Haiku Society
79 Westbury Rd
Barking
Essex IG11 7PL

Website: http://britishhaikusociety.org.uk/

Printed by:
Direct Services Ltd
www.directservices.bg
Todor Todorov
gsm: +359 886 101016

This book is printed on Xerox iGEN platform – for more information please visit www.xerox.com